Breaking Boundaries:

Employee engagement through the Principles of Greatness

---

10 Easy steps to build employee engagement with your team AND create a great place to work

HR Bites Series: Book 1

by

Adele Marsh MCIPD

Published in Great Britain by: My HRBP Publishing

ISBN-13:978-1530525027

ISBN-10:1530525020

Printed in the United Kingdom First Printing, 2016

My HRBP Publishing

My HR Business Partner Publishing

www.myhrbusinesspartner.co.uk

info@myhrbusinesspartner.co.uk

Table of Contents

Introduction – The Cycle of Disengagement...............................6

So what's changed in the last 20 years? 11

Where are we now?...17

What is employee engagement really about? 23

How do you go about creating a culture of engagement? 27

Breaking Boundaries: Behind the Principles of Greatness.......29

Introducing the Principles of Greatness...................................39

Applying the Principles of Greatness in the workplace 47

What is your doctrine? 72

Conclusion..74

Additional Resources 78

Author Thank You 79

About the Author...80

References 82

Introduction – The Cycle of Disengagement

No matter what industry you are in, I am sure that at least once in your professional life you have come across a disengaged workplace. For those of you reading this whom have worked across multiple businesses or multiples sectors in your career, you may have come across many disengaged workplaces; your key reason for moving on from one workplace to another may have been the unhappiness of the previous workplace.

The term employee engagement was coined in the 90s and has become the forefront of human resource practices today; it is no longer sufficient to employ employees, now you have to engage with them if you want to keep them happy and hang on to them.

During my professional life I have had the pleasure of working in some extremely busy, almost relentless workplaces, yet somehow nearly everyone was engaged; I've also worked in some businesses where the pace of work was relatively relaxed and yet everyone was moaning and no one was happy. I've also been on the receiving end where as an employee I was very disengaged and frustrated, in fact that very reason saw me move from one particular employer pronto!

The problem of creating an engaged workforce often lands at the feet of management or HR, but in this book I will show you how the problem lies with everyone in the workplace and I will show you what part everyone has to play in fixing the problem.

Management and employees must both contribute to engagement.

What is the difference between a happy workforce and an engaged workforce?

You might think that a happy workforce is an engaged workforce, well actually no, the 2 things are not necessarily the same thing. You might find that some employees are happy: happy with their salary, happy with their working hours, happy with their line manager, happy with the colleagues they work with – they work hard, stay loyal and don't leave the company. But are they engaged?

What is being engaged?

Being engaged means being so embedded in the organisation and the work they do, that employees are actively contributing every day to move the organisation forward, improve sales, gain/retain customers and literally going over and above the call of duty. A happy employee does not necessarily go over and above, so they aren't necessarily engaged. If you have happy but not engaged employees, they might resist attempts at change as they won't want anything to change their current state of happiness and you might find problems moving your business forward; they might just get stuck in their ways.

Why might an employee be happy and not engaged?

Well Penny Loveless, director of Pecan Partnership says 1) Lack of awareness,
2) Lack of belief and
3) It's easier to stay in denial and smile. [i]

However, having a happy workforce that isn't engaged is not exactly a bad problem to have, at least you can work up some ideas to improve engagement and generally start to encourage them towards it.

If you have an unhappy workforce that is completely disengaged, then you probably have a huge problem with your workplace culture and a larger mountain to climb. That being said, nothing is impossible and after reading this book you should have some inspiration on what to do next.

Imagine you have that awful situation of an unhappy workforce. Why should you want to fix this problem?

Why is an unhappy workforce a problem?

Well firstly, no one likes sitting around listening to people moaning, whinging, whining and complaining. Whether it be in the morning around the coffee machine or in the 'have you got 5 minutes?' request for a quick chat that turns into a two-hour moaning session; I am sure no one actually enjoys hearing the moaning!

You see, once the moaning is over there is actually a serious part that comes with addressing the issue.

You will need to investigate, identify and fix the problem that's been raised. This takes time, money and resources, distracting the relevant manager / HR person / co-worker from other activities. Ignoring the problem only leads to it festering away until it becomes worse and often unbearable.

What happens if that complaint actually becomes a formal grievance?

Well, then you've got a whole realm of formal processes, meetings and outcomes that will follow, a most unpleasant atmosphere whilst all this is going on and you must not forget that the 'accused' in the scenario is also an employee who, despite their alleged actions, needs consideration.

Once the seed of unhappiness is sewn it spreads, from a minor moan to a formal grievance; from a couple of small whinges about a colleague or manager to a formal complaint of bullying and harassment, and let's not forget how accessible services such as ACAS are to employees and before you know it, you might have a case of constructive dismissal and be heading towards an employment tribunal. This all becomes a very nasty, expensive situation.

It's not just the employees implicated in the scenario; employees talk, no matter how much you say 'keep this matter to yourself' it won't happen. A workplace is like Chinese whispers, before you know it the whole team is involved and everyone has an opinion.

So what's the end result?

Unhappiness can most certainly lead to disengagement.

Disengagement then becomes a cycle. A disengaged workplace = lower productivity = higher employee relations issues (grievances and disciplinaries) = more leavers = more recruitment = more training = lower capacity to produce results = less customer satisfaction = more pressure on the rest of the team = more stress = more leavers = you have no business left!

Breaking the Cycle of Disengagement

We need to break the cycle of disengagement. I believe there are 3 key steps to doing this:

Step 1: Create happiness in your workforce

Step 2: Move them happiness to engagement

Step 3: Keep them engaged

This book is a simple guide to instilling a culture that everyone can abide by. No HR Degree is needed, it's not rocket science, just some simple guidelines and for ensuring your workplace is on the path to happiness, then engagement and finally staying engaged.

So what's changed in the last 20 years?

Over the last 20 years there has been a huge shift in the way that we look at human resources: even just the term itself has evolved from personnel to human resource management, human capital and human resource development.

HR professionals will tell you an in depth and complex HRD strategy is needed to succeed as an organisation grows; I myself have written hundreds of pages into a strategy, adopting pillars / goals / drivers / framework / policies and processes.

This may be true in some businesses, but what a lot of the research I find in human resource management books fails to talk about is the basics of human nature. You can have the best documented policies, procedures and plans but if the human beings in your business can't be civilised, respectful and communicative with each other, then none of your strategy is going to work.

How do you engage employees in a meaningful way?

In order to engage employees in a meaningful way, retain them from absconding to your competitors and reap the rewards of a high performance work culture and grow our businesses (which I am guessing is probably your ultimate goal) you need to set out your doctrine.

Your doctrine is as simple as "The basis of how we do business". The absolute basics of how you want each and every individual within your organisation to go about their day to day being within the workplace.

From the cleaner, warehouse operative, customer service advisor, team leader, management, head of department, senior executive to the CEO, no one is immune. The doctrine is essentially to keeping peace, harmony and happiness. The doctrine that I believe in is formulated around the Principles of Greatness.

Once you implement the Principles of Greatness (and satisfy a few hygiene factors), you will spread the happiness disease, give people the right environment to let them flourish and succeed, then break the cycle of disengagement. The Principles of Greatness don't just apply to the workplace. If everyone in the world could just stop and think for a moment about this simple framework, then I believe the world would be a much happier place. But before I go about solving world peace I shall just try to point a few business leaders in the right direction!

So what's new?

In recent years, employee expectation has become higher and higher. Be under no illusion that employees want financial and emotional reward at work, and one size does not fit all. We now have 3 to 4 generations in the workforce, all with different expectations. Just managing across the generation gaps is a challenge in itself.

I remember implementing a performance related bonus scheme in a customer service environment and took great care to make sure that not only were there rewards for the highest performers but also the most improved each month, what I felt we offered was an inclusive reward scheme for the whole team.

When sitting with a team member in a one-to-one (a couple of months shortly after the scheme was launched) this particular team member fed back to me that since the introduction of the scheme they were completely demotivated in their role, they had never felt so demotivated as since the scheme was put in place. I had managed to upset and unsettle a perfectly good worker who was achieving all her daily targets, with whom I did not have any performance concerns but who had taken a completely different view of the performance related bonuses. I was mortified!

I talked over the new scheme with this employee, I sought feedback from others in the team, I empowered her to have a voice on the matter and work alongside me to find other incentives that appealed to the rest of the team and from this the whole team felt valued, included and part of the greater picture.

Ultimately they all improved their productivity because they all felt they had something to offer, just in different ways. Some were never going to work faster or produce more output but they contributed to improvements in quality or initiating new ideas or kept up the team morale. Each team member then benefitted from the scheme in a different way.

Why is engagement not about driving performance?

Engagement is not about dangling as many juicy carrots as possible and hoping that everyone chomps their way through them. If you do that, what happens when the carrots are all eaten up? Will everyone be satisfied? Will they stay performing in over drive or will they take their foot of the gas and relax until you find a bigger carrot to dangle next time?

You don't want a stop / start approach to performance. You want a continually high performing team that is always striving for excellence but without you dangling huge bunches of carrots in front of them! Engagement is about creating a culture that allows people to thrive, develop, learn, flourish and achieve. Engagement enables a place to exist where high performance comes naturally.

Employee engagement is not a huge secret, though many of my HR colleagues would have you believe. If you apply a little thought to the ideas I give you in this book you will have initiated a whole employee engagement programme without even knowing it.

There is no need for expensive external consultants, no need for managers to be tied up in delivery of long winded complicated initiatives. What I offer you is 10 guiding principles that you can take straight back to your organisation, no matter how big or small, and start that change.

So why can't you 'motivate' an employee?

For years we have relied on motivational theories based on the work of Maslow, McGregor, Hertz, McClelland and Vroom. (if you want to know more about these, checkout this simple summary here: (http://www.yourcoach.be/en/employee-motivation-theories/). Put *extremely* simply, we have learned from these theorists is that in order to be motivated, some basic fundamental needs (explained in each theory) must be met.

So in the last 5 years, the latest shift in employee engagement is the understanding that maybe you cannot actually motivate an employee, they are already motivated. This shift is the most significant in the last 30 years. How often have you heard managers looking for new ways to motivate and incentivise employees to 'perform', but now we are finding that people are already motivated, just by different factors.

Autonomy, Relatedness and Competence

In her book "*Why Motivating People Doesn't Work . . . and What Does: The New Science of Leading, Energizing, and Engaging*", Susan Fowler explains beautifully in 3 simple words which psychological needs must be met in each workplace in order to achieve an engaged workforce:

Autonomy, Relatedness and Competence (ARC)[ii]

"Autonomy is our human need to perceive we have choices. It is our need to feel that what we are doing is of our own volition. It is our perception that we are the source of our actions"

"Relatedness is our need to care about and be cared about by others. It is our need to feel connected to others without concerns about ulterior motives. It is our need to feel that we are contributing to something greater than ourselves"

"Competence is our need to feel effective at meeting everyday challenges and opportunities. It is demonstrating skill over time. It is feeling a sense of growth and flourishing."[iii]

I would emphatically urge you to read Susan Fowler's book for a deeper understanding of what it means to satisfy Autonomy, Relatedness and Competence (ARC) in the workplace.

She explains how we all have a psychological need to learn, grow, develop, contribute, to be part of a social situation and how business leaders can hinder this by traditional motivational techniques and taking away an environment conducive to these elements.

What can be worse still, is when you undermine competence in people at work, you tend to affect other aspects of their life. Since most people spend around 75% of their lives doing something connected with their work (either being at work, travelling to work, training for work, socialising with work colleagues, and so on) if their ARC psychological needs are not being satisfied it can have a wider impact on their lives outside work.

Do you really want to be responsible for an employee's marriage break up because their disengagement at work had such an impact on their home life? Do you think about that completely disagreeable employee who goes home every day to take out their frustrations on other family members?

We need to stop supplying our employees with 'motivational junk food' and instead we need to look to satisfy psychological needs and provide an environment where each employee can thrive...

humans have a desire to thrive, grow and develop. But how many organisations still incentivise their managers related to performance?

Where are we now?

"Today, more than twice as many employees are motivated by work passion than career ambition (12 percent vs. 5 percent), indicating a need for leadership to focus on making the work environment compelling and enjoyable for everyone" [iv]

We have an engagement deficit... it's official!

In 2009 Kenexa reported that the UK had an employee engagement deficit, that around only 33% of the UK workers were engaged and the UK was ranked 9th for engagement of the world's 12 largest economies by GDP.

The UK also has a productivity deficit. In 2011 an ONS survey found that output per hour in the UK was 15% below the average for the rest of the G7 industrialised nations; on an output per worker basis, UK productivity was 20% lower than the rest of the G7 in 2011. This represented the widest productivity gap since 1995.

By 2014 the ONS found that output per hour had decreased even further and was now 20 % lower than the rest of the G7 nations. The UK had a "productivity gap" of about 18% compared with a gap of about 7% for the rest of the G7.

In Deloitte's Human Capital Trends survey 2015, more than 50% of the respondents had either no programme for employee engagement or at best a poor programme. Considering the worsening statistics of productivity in the UK, and knowing how important employee engagement is for productivity and business success it is quite a frightening statistic.

In Spring 2015 the CIPD reported their Employee Outlook survey showing that 39% of employees were engaged, just over 2% were disengaged and just under 59% were neutral.[v] That shows a very large risk to UK businesses when 60% of your workforce is not engaged.

We need to focus on culture

The losers in this ever more competitive business environment or those organisations who fail to recognise that employee engagement is at an all-time low. Equally, there are those that try to solve this problem by placing focus on 'motivating' employees in order to gain employee engagement.

What do I mean by that? I mean those organisations who are trying to dangle those huge carrots that don't work; those trying to 'motivate' employees with promises of reward that might work in the short term, but won't work in the long term.

The winners in this ever changing situation over the last 15 years have been the organisations that embrace employee happiness and take time to understand why an employee is motivated already, and what quality of motivation exists, not what initiatives the organisation can impose 'to motivate' the employee.

Remember, step 1 is creating a happy workforce, step 2 is engaging with them and step 3 is keeping them engaged.

You do not need to 'find' ways to motivate an employee. Employees are already motivated by the need to learn, the need to progress, the need to earn money, the need to socialise with others and more. You just need to provide a platform and environment where those motivations can exist and flourish, the employees will do the rest.

Those organisations who understand that employee engagement is about culture, not motivation, are seeing the positive effects on levels of absenteeism, retention, levels of innovation, customer service, positive outcomes in public services and on staff advocacy of their organisations. Employer branding is going to play a very large part with organisations in the next few years, so you want to make sure your organisation has got it right!

Those organisations that allow employees to have fun at work, to play on the pool table, to have a game of office basketball, to get up whenever they want and go for a jog around the block to reenergise, who provide gym memberships and a basket of fruit each day. It is those organisations that see greater commitment. Employees respect that fact that they are being giving autonomy over their working day, they are not being micro managed. As long as they meet their project / output delivery goals then it doesn't matter how they organise their working day.

I personally work in overdrive first thing in the morning. Allow me to get up at 6am and work furiously over a couple of coffees before getting dressed, then let me go work out at the gym around 9.30am and come back to my desk at 11am and I am on fire! But everyone is different.

Giving them the flexibility to work from home, work from the coffee shop, the breakout area, the train or wherever they want is often key to increasing productivity. Letting them take natural breaks throughout the day when *their* body tells them to, not when the office clock says they should.

It is also clear that engagement impacts more on performance than the other way around. A study in a leading retail bank found that employee engagement levels predicted subsequent business level performance over a 3-year horizon, while business unit performance predicted engagement only over a single year.

Is your business a great place to work?

A Great Place to Work (http://www.greatplacetowork.co.uk/) publishes top UK and multinationals that have ranked amongst the best companies to work for. At the core of their success in the listings is the fact that "central to employees' perception of a great culture were camaraderie factors" as well as the value put on "competent management, including leaders' effectiveness at coordinating staff".vi

It may be no surprise to hear that Google was #1 in the rankings of the best global business to work for.

A Great Place to Work identifies 9 key areas a business needs to focus on to create a truly excellent culture:

1) Inspiring
2) Hiring
3) Welcoming
4) Caring
5) Listening
6) Thanking
7) Sharing
8) Celebrating
9) Developing

(http://www.greatplacetowork.co.uk/our-services/assess-your-organisation/workplace-culture-assessment) [vii]

If you truly want to make your business a great place to work, then I challenge you to sign up to the UK's Best Workplaces Programme and have your business assessed. Even if it's not quite where it needs to be right now, you will be working towards a great framework that will keep you on the path to success.

What is employee engagement really about?

Employee engagement may be the phrase that has become widely used over the last 20 years, but it is nothing new. Keeping your workforce engaged has been the key element to successful businesses the world over for decades.

ACAS describe employee engagement as having 4 key ingredients for a "happier, more motivated and more productive workforce" as:

1. leaders with a vision who value how individuals contribute
2. line managers who empower rather than control their staff
3. values that are lived and not just spoken, leading to a sense of trust and integrity
4. employees who have the chance to voice their views and concerns.

I highly recommend that you take a look at the Engage for Success website (http://engageforsuccess.org/what-is-employee-engagement). They define employee engagement with extreme clarity and simplicity:

"Employee engagement is a workplace approach resulting in the right conditions for all members of an organisation to give of their best each day, committed to their organisation's goals and values, motivated to contribute to organisational success, with an enhanced sense of their own well-being."

I could spend the next few chapters wittering on about what employee engagement is, but put simply it's about a workforce that wakes up every morning with the desire to go to work, to do their best and be part of a great organisation that values them. Employee engagement is about an organisation that focuses all its' efforts around the employees.

Employee engagement is not about HR initiative after initiative, it's about a culture, a way of being every day, a way of working harmoniously with colleagues, respecting each other and contributing to the organisation's success. Employee engagement has been the recent priority of the modern HR professionals, coined by management theorists for the last 20 years as the new way forward and spawning many an expensive training programmes and leadership initiatives.

The good news is that you CAN improve employee engagement in your organisation; you CAN make the shift towards a happy, motivated and engaged workforce; it is never too late to make the change. You CAN make your workplace a great place to work.

The following chapters will give you an introduction to the Principles of Greatness and why they are relevant to employee engagement in the modern workplace.

Additional resources in the Appendices will point you in the right direction for further help.

"Organizations that create a culture defined by meaningful work, deep employee engagement, job and organizational fit, and strong leadership are outperforming their peers and will likely beat their competition in attracting top talent."

Deloitte 2015

How do you go about creating a culture of engagement?

If you're in the process of creating a new business then you can start from scratch, fantastic, but what if you're in an existing organisation and you're going to need to change everyone's mind-set? Well it won't be easy.

First you will need to get everyone to 'buy-in' to the new way of doing things. How exactly you do that in your individual organisation will be up to you to decide, but the most important thing to remember when you've read this book and want to go rushing off is that you will have to explain the principles of ARC (satisfying your colleagues' needs for psychological growth and interaction through Autonomy, Relatedness and Competence) and also making managers understand that motivating employees does not work, and worse still can have a negative effect of demotivating them. If you do nothing else but insist that all your managers read Susan Fowler's book, then you will definitely be heading in the right direction!

However, that's not all I want you to do! I want you to embrace the simple ideas I put forward to you in this book, to interpret them for your own organisation, to do further research with the resources I recommend and go forward as a great leader.

If you can learn to apply the Principles of Greatness then you will be on the right path, you will halve your learning curve (and when you are running a business your time is precious). You will cut out some of the mistakes and have your people following you to wherever you want to take them. You will have a basic but solid framework from which you can grow your business and engage your people.

Breaking Boundaries: Behind the Principles of Greatness

So who am I and why should you be reading this?

My name is Adele Marsh and I am an HR Consultant and Chartered Member of the CIPD. My company is called "My HR Business Partner" and I help SMEs in the UK with their human resource management.

I have over 15 years of operational management experience in the late night leisure, licensed trade and contact centre industries. I've also worked in ecommerce, construction and a private Company delivering public sector employability contracts. I know many different challenges business owners and managers face every day with their people because I have been there.

I have managed direct teams of up to 250 people as an HR Operations Director with a start-up that grew to over £1.1m turnover in just over 3 years. I managed a team of Area Managers, developed a bespoke Management Development programme and created a Human Resource Development strategy.

Our business was based in 90 locations around the UK and we didn't have one formal office premise. All managers and directors worked remotely from home, we totally embraced the modern technologies and new ways of working and trusted our people to be doing what they were supposed to be doing.

Following 5 years with this business I decided it was time to move on and I really wanted to specialise in Human Resource Management and undertook my Professional Assessment of Competence Level 7 (post graduate) qualification with the CIPD to gain Chartered Membership in 2012.

I then spent 18 months in Northern Ireland as a successful HR Business Partner for a global contact centre organisation employing over 130,000 staff across 258 sites. I had HR responsibilities for nearly 450 employees.

Moving back to England towards the end of 2013, I spent 6 months as an HR Consultant for and HR Consultancy agency before deciding to go it alone founding My HR Business Partner. My USP for My HR Business Partner is that I actually want to get involved fully with each business. I like to think strategically about adding value, not just processing the HR paperwork! During my time with the HR consultancy agency I found that just answering the phone and giving the relevant HR legal advice wasn't enough. I like to get involved with people.

At school I had a keen interest in the classics, studying Latin, Greek and Roman Mythology and Philosophy. So you might find me referring to some of these as I move through this book. I have danced all my life, I'm a qualified dance and fitness instructor and I hold regular classes and performances.

My first Human Resource Development strategy

As I mentioned earlier, during my time with the start-up I created my first Human Resource Development strategy, built on 4 Pillars:

1 Nurturing Talent,

2 Demonstrating excellent leadership,

3 Setting the appropriate climate,

4 Driving Performance

I quickly realised that my Area Managers and remote trainers were the linchpins of our business. Without them we would not have survived. I was very proud of the fact that most of them had been promoted (quite quickly) from within the business and were originally members of the sales or customer service staff. We felt privileged that we had a lot of raw talent, but at the same time challenged because that's exactly what it was, RAW talent. It needed refining!

So I created 2 programmes. The first was an Area Trainer's programme, essentially a 'train the trainer format' which was very successful. The second was a Management Development programme for my Area Managers. This included monthly training workshops / coaching / mentoring / supporting the Area Managers.

On one particular training occasion I facilitated a discussion, and a question came out of the discussion around being successful, and the question was asked of how do you become successful? One of the first responses that came from a team member was that you needed confidence.

Without confidence you won't even put a foot forward and start doing anything that moves you towards success.

So what is confidence and how do you become confident?

Well this was something I had never struggled with. I had never had a problem walking into a room full of Directors and presenting my ideas, or standing at a conference presenting.

In my spare time as a Dance and Fitness instructor, I teach in front of large groups of people and have never had an issue with holding an audience and of course performing, on a stage in front of hundreds of people... no problem!

This did however set me thinking, because whilst talking to various people about various things I have done or achieved I have often heard 'well I wouldn't have the confidence to do that' or 'I wouldn't have the confidence to go there on my own'.

A few examples which have surprised me were people (and more so from ladies) saying they would never go travelling on their own, they would never walk into a pub or club on their own, they couldn't speak in front of an audience, they wouldn't ask a man to dance at a social function.

So what gave me that confidence? This appeared a simple question, but as I hadn't struggled with it, it wasn't something I was aware that I had in abundance and others were wanting what I had!

After some thought though I realised that from a very early age I had belief... I had belief in myself, belief in the way that I do things, belief in my own ability to succeed in whatever I do, and that inward belief presents itself outwardly as confidence.

Belief is looking in the mirror each day and saying "I can, I will, no one will stop me"

The Confidence Cycle

So when you have confidence, it opens up other doors, it helps you in the way that you tackle life. In business and in your social life the more confidence you have, the more doors you open, because everything becomes achievable.

Sometimes you lack direction, but never the attack. Having confidence gives you ambition which helps you set higher goals, which gives you the motivation to succeed and the more you succeed the more confidence you get.

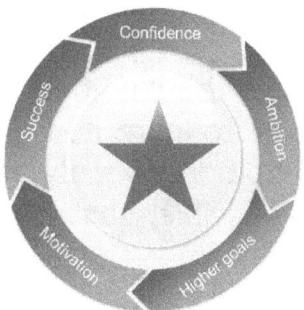

Take a look at the Confidence Cycle.[viii] Once you have confidence you grow ambition, then you start setting yourself higher goals, you reach those goals and this gives you more motivation to succeed, you have success which in turns grows your confidence even further and before you know it you've grown and grown.

So what stops people from achieving? Often it's the lack of confidence or the self-belief. So if you have confidence, fantastic; but what if you don't? Something I have always been passionate about is inspiring other people. If I can give someone else the confidence to succeed, then I have succeeded further.

One of the questions I ask when recruiting for a management position, is 'Tell me about someone you have inspired or developed to succeed; where were they when you found them, where are they now and how did you help them to get there?'

It is important that we share our experiences and inspire other people. In learning to grow ourselves we need to support, share and inspire each other to help everyone succeed.

We need to remember that creating a culture of engagement means having belief in ourselves and others. It means inspiring them to succeed. We need to give our employees the confidence to move on and up, to try new things, to learn new skills to have higher goals and ambition, to truly go where they never thought was possible, such as the shop floor team member that becomes the CEO in 15 years' time.

One such notable person that's done just that in her career is Martina Navratilova. The famous tennis player was World No. 1 for a total of 332 weeks in singles, and a record 237 weeks in doubles, making her the only player in history to have held the top spot in both singles and doubles for over 200 weeks.

She won 18 Grand Slam singles titles, 31 major women's doubles titles (an all-time record), and 10 major mixed doubles titles. She reached the Wimbledon singles final 12 times, including nine consecutive years from 1982 through 1990, and won the women's singles title at Wimbledon a record nine times.

She and Billie Jean King each won 20 Wimbledon titles, an all-time record. Navratilova is one of just three women to have accomplished a career Grand Slam in singles, women's doubles, and mixed doubles (called the Grand Slam "boxed set")

I came across a clip of Martina Navratilova speaking at the BBC 100 Women conference. Here, Martina explains the challenges she faced in the Czech Republic, and how she had to leave to seek American Citizenship, not being able to return home for 5 years. She had to hide her sexuality in order to gain American citizenship (as this was a disqualifier for citizenship at the time). But she sacrificed these things in order to achieve.

3 things that Martina very poignantly touches on are:

1 Breaking Boundaries

2 Belief in yourself

3 and Being yourself...

(watch Martina speaking about these here: https://www.youtube.com/watch?v=jZTaNq2xvZ8)

This struck a chord with me, because when I came across this clip on YouTube in about May 2014 I remembered the Management Development Programme from the start-up 4 years before. Whilst creating this I had put together a poster, called 'Breaking Boundaries' which was about 10 key steps to creating a high performance culture.

'Breaking Boundaries' was about instilling the Principles of Greatness, believing in yourself and others and allowing people to be themselves but the best selves that they can be. 'Breaking Boundaries' was and attempt to articulate a great workplace culture.

Now although this was intended for the workplace it was explaining how by instilling some very basic principles (that I believe we all have within us), that we could create a workplace where people thrived. A workplace where people actually wanted to come to work each day and give it their best shot. We could create somewhere where creativity was in abundance and negativity a thing of the past. We could create a workplace where people believed in themselves, others believed in them, they could break boundaries and be themselves, just like Martina's message.

I felt that I had a great message to give. I felt my message was not only for the workplace but also relevant to all aspects of life. I felt that if someone could go about applying the 'Principles of Greatness' to everything they do that they would live a much more enriched existence.

Now by 'Greatness' I don't mean being financially rich or famous. I mean that when you achieve greatness it is because you have helped others to succeed, you've shown compassion for a stranger, you've inspired a child, you've given a colleague a vision to solve a problem, you've imparted your wisdom in some way. There are many ways to interpret 'Greatness', but a truly 'great' person is someone who has shown others how to succeed, someone who has served others. Becoming a servant leader in today's modern business I believe is the way forward.

Introducing the Principles of Greatness

Certain types of 'greatness' (normally financial and how to achieve them), have been widely written about in recent times with many a self-help book showing the enlightened reader the path to achieving greatness and success in life.

The 10 Principles of Greatness are a simple way of being, that's it... just a way to go about your everyday life with these 10 principles in mind and greatness will follow you.

It is not just about where you get to in life, but how you got there too. My guidance is mainly about being a good human being and making sure you are being that every day. These 10 simple words that you should strive to personify may open up the door to success if you're a manager or business owner, but also in whatever it is you want to achieve: baking a cake, walking down the road, painting a masterpiece, writing a book, achieving a promotion, for example.

I truly believe that principles such as these can guide us through all aspects of our lives.

Why 10 Principles of Greatness?

For the purposes of the workplace I suggest the following 10 Principles of Greatness are foundations, they on their own do not make a business successful; but a strong business is built on great foundations.

Enlightening your workforce to these principles is the first foundation. Ensuring that they are striving to live and work with these principles in mind and that the workplace is filled with like-minded people is the second step to a work environment that is receptive to creativity, autonomy and where people can experience relatedness.

Once you have achieved this the workforce becomes relaxed, they feel valued and ready to give you their dedication, their creativity and they will go on to build a great business, together.

By following these 10 foundations you will build a strong, ethical and successful business. Folowing these principles will help your business go from strength to strength.

You must put worth and value on yourself, your employees, your friends and family. Enlighten them to the Principles of Greatness and help them live, breathe and work to those principles every day.

So here's an overview (the following chapters explain in much further detail).

1: Values

What are values and why are they important? We can think of values as choices regarding an appropriate course of action. Values reflect a person's way of behaving and attitude towards being. Some values are inherently intrinsic, yet others are shaped by experience and can be swayed by evidence or argument.

At the core of all of us should be our values; think that's cliché? Well maybe, but if you don't have values then how will anyone around you?

So what are the core values for each of us? Well I believe I can simplify this to just 5. If these 5 are the life and breathe of the way you go about your daily business, then you will begin to see the difference around you:

Trust... empower everyone, trust them to make the right decisions, don't dictate to them

Honesty... be honest with each other, without fear of retribution

Kindness... recognise and celebrate differences, support each other, make acts of kindness everyday occurrences

Fairness... be fair and consistent in your approach

Respect... show respect to everyone, make sure you earn your respect through your actions, don't just expect respect from others

These values are your ethics, your conscience of how you conduct yourself and your business. Your values determine how you go about day to day, how you demonstrate your standards. When each and every one of us can learn to be kind to each other, to respect each other's opinions, to learn from one another, to trust people around us and be empowered to make our own decisions, then we will grow and thrive.

In the workplace, when managers can be honest with employees (and vice versa) and demonstrate fairness with their actions, when every employee no matter what level within the business feels they are valued as much as any other employee, then harmony will exist.

2: Desire

Having the desire to do something, to achieve something is half the battle. If you have desire you have will, you have intent, you have a longing for that object or that something to happen. All humans have basic desires for physiological fulfilment: you need to feel warmth, you need to feel full after a meal, you need to feel emotional connections with other human beings, to be socially accepted and, many more. However, desire is far more than that. Without desire and the need to feel satisfied in some way we are not human, there is pleasure in achieving or obtaining whatever it is we desire.

3: Passion

Passion can be described as a compelling emotion or enthusiasm for something or someone. It is an intense emotion. People experience passions for pleasure, learning, discovery, other times it can be for your work. Someone who feels passionately about their work will work harder whilst striving to feel satisfaction from their work. Passion is a motivator. Higher levels of psychological wellbeing can be experienced by those who are passionate about the activity or work that they are doing. Passion and Desire are deeply connected, practically inseparable according to Plato and Aristotle. Passion can be both positive and negative.

4: Vision

Having vision is having the capacity or foresight to envisage the possibilities in your future and plan accordingly, if you so desire to achieve this future. To have a vision is to have a goal, to be focused on a desired outcome. It doesn't matter how small or big your vision is, but if you don't have a vision then what is it you are working towards in your personal life, your professional life, your leisure activities? Creating your vision helps you plan towards attaining your future. It helps you map out what you need to do to get there.

5: Courage

Having courage is having the ability to do something that frightens you, or at least makes you feel very uncomfortable. It is the ability to do something that no one else thinks you can do. It is the strength in your character that says you will overcome that fear. It is having the ability to act on your beliefs, to follow your vision (no matter how crazy others tell you that you might be). The word encourage is the act of others to persuade someone to do something, it can be a way of talking or behaving that gives someone the confidence to do something that they fear or feel apprehensive about.

6: Belief

To have belief is to have trust and confidence in something or someone. Belief doesn't mean having proof that something exists, it's having the faith that it exists without the empirical proof. Having belief in someone occurs when that person has earned your respect, your trust and they have demonstrated their integrity to you. To have belief in yourself is to have confidence that you will succeed. To gain others' belief you must build trust and confidence.

7: Fortitude

When someone is described as having fortitude it means they have the emotional resilience or strength of mind to deal with a difficult situation. By being able to withstand adversity and come out stronger without the damaging of one's spirit then it can be said that one has fortitude. Fortitude is essential for survival in today's modern world.

8: Compassion

To demonstrate compassion is to show concern for the misfortune of others, to have empathy and to care about what happens. When one shows compassion one is showing their humanity and kindness. When one puts compassion for others before their own needs then one becomes selfless.

9: Integrity

Acting with integrity every day demonstrates your trustworthiness. Doing the right thing, being honest, having ethics and principles shows that you have integrity. Always delivering on your promises and being sincere with others shows your integrity.

10: Wisdom

To have wisdom, one must first have knowledge and experience of their subject, one must then use this knowledge and experience to act with sound judgement.

"In short, wisdom is a disposition to find the truth coupled with an optimum judgement as to what actions should be taken." [ix]

In summary:

Having established the foundations for our success we need to live by them every day. So how do we do that? Well, from the moment we wake up to the moment we fall asleep, we live, breathe and share. There is no greater strength than the strength of people together.

What principles of greatness are you walking in?

Working hard, learning, respecting others, listening, never giving up and continually striving to do better will make you succeed. Take the time to study and embed these initial 10 Principles of Greatness in your life as your starting foundation for success.

Even if you just take away one thought or initiative from this book and it helps you make a positive change in your life or work then I have succeeded.

Remember you are trying to develop a captivating, vivacious environment where your employees are positively engaged.

"I love those who can smile in trouble, who can gather strength from distress, and grow brave by reflection. 'Tis the business of little minds to shrink, but they whose heart is firm, and whose conscience approves their conduct, will pursue their principles unto death."

Leonardo de Vinci

Applying the Principles of Greatness in the workplace

I will show you that the formula for success has just 10 simple ingredients. 10 steps to creating an absolutely awesome workplace... So let's get started!

Step 1: Set out your values

What's the first thought that comes to mind when you mention setting standards in a business? Is it policies, procedures, guidelines, employee handbooks?

Well over the last 40 years it might well have been. The HR professionals and managers would have spent hours creating those policies and delivering them out to the workforce. You will also find guidelines on what happens when an employee doesn't meet those standards, the consequences of poor performance or conduct which normally result in a disciplinary process or in more serious cases, dismissal.

But why on earth would you go to all that trouble to recruit, train and develop someone simply for them to be booted out the door when their performance or conduct lapses? Did you ever stop to think why that person was great at the start and has since developed poor behaviours? Surely they weren't like that at the beginning or you wouldn't have employed them, would you?

How would it be if you didn't even have a disciplinary policy because you were absolutely sure that none of your employees would ever find themselves in a situation where they might fall short of it?

Now I am not suggesting you can just throw your disciplinary procedure out the window (since having a disciplinary policy is still a statutory requirement in the UK as of 2016, you can't just throw it out!); but imagine your business had such strong core values, that you *could* throw out your disciplinary policy and replace this with a vision statement such as this:

'We expect every colleague to do their best, to give 110% of their effort every day to their tasks, their team and their managers. In return we will give every colleague the opportunity to thrive, flourish and excel, to follow their dreams and be part of a great organisation.

We expect everyone to respect each other and to act appropriately and professionally at all times. With mutual respect we can work in a harmonious environment without the need for written rules and regulations as we believe all our colleagues have it within them to work professionally with the people around them.

If you feel that you are not able to perform effectively in your role we encourage you to discuss this with your manager and colleagues so that you may be given the support you need to succeed. When it is time to move on, we extend the mutuality of trust that you will know when to walk away with your head held high saying I gave it my best, I have learned valuable skills which I can take forward to the next chapter in my life and I leave behind great friends but take with me great friendships forever.'

Wouldn't that be a great a statement!

In my years as an HR professional I have worked in some interesting organisations. In one organisation we had a rule for just about everything, in particular we had a dress code which was very prescriptive. Your skirt had to be below the knee, your blouse could not be sleeveless with your armpits on display, you could not wear denim, open toed shoes and so on.

So what was the purpose of this? We didn't work in a customer facing environment so no one other than colleagues would see the way we looked; we did not work in a manufacturing environment with health and safety considerations in relations to machinery; we did not have a particularly ethnically diverse workforce so religious dress observances weren't an issue, so why? I never did get to the bottom of it!!

The point about this was that it 'just was'; it was written into the employee handbook and there it was, and of course there was the obligatory disciplinary consequences of not adhering to the policy. The HR team were nicknamed the 'fashion police' since we had to issue a 'conversation recorder' for anyone who didn't comply and then promptly send them home.

So there you are on a busy day, customer service falling below expectation and the team short on resource because you sent their colleague home and for what? Because their skirt was 1/2 an inch above the knee!!

Why can't we trust employees to make informed decisions about their conduct in the workplace? Well I believe this happens when we haven't instilled our values or worse still we haven't even thought about or set out our values, even if we have them tucked away somewhere.

If we set out our values and everyone understands them, lives and breathes them, then why should you even need a disciplinary policy?

The point I am trying to make is that we should be making a shift towards values and empowerment, empowering our employees to make the right choices by themselves, not because we create a set of rules for them. I believe any business can achieve this.

When businesses talk about setting standards they should really be talking about setting out their values. It's not about setting up a set of rules, it's about creating an atmosphere and culture where everyone has values. Everyone values high standards in their work, their conduct, their behaviour; where respect and understanding of each other is at the forefront.

At the core of any organisation should be the organisation's values, if *you* don't have values then how will your employees? In the previous chapter I gave you an overview of the Principles of Greatness and I set out 5 core values. Let's remind ourselves again:

Trust, Honesty, Kindness, Fairness, Respect

If these 5 are the life and breathe of your organisation you will begin to see the difference in your workplace. These values are your ethics, your conscience of how you conduct yourself and your business. Your values determine how you do business, how your employees demonstrate their standards. When each and every one of your employees can learn to be kind to each other, to respect each other's opinions and learn from one another, to trust senior management and be empowered to make their own decisions, employees grow within the business and thrive.

In 2014 the Great Place to Work organisation surveyed the 100 Companies that made it to the top of the 'Best Places to Work' list. 97% of these said they had statements about their values, and that these values were absolutely integral to their business success. 3% said that although they had no formal values written down that they still had guiding principles. You can read the full report here[x]:

http://www.greatplacetowork.co.uk/storage/document s/organisational%20values%20are%20they%20worth %20the%20bother%20final2%20web%20031114.pdf

So remember:
   1) Set out your values (Trust, Honesty, Kindness, Fairness and Respect as your starting point)
   2) Share your values
   3) Instil your values throughout the workplace
   4) Be proud of your values
   5) Shout about your values

Step 2: Share your desires

Desire in the workplace can be seen as employees who desire to be there, those who desire a particular career path, a promotion, to create a new project, to become a leader. Often as managers we forget to ask employees what they actually desire. It might not always be the answer we want to hear and it might actually be something that is completely impractical or not achievable, but we shouldn't dismiss it.

Learning what *you* as a business leader and your employees desire can add great value to creative processes; it can give new ideas to team structure, to new projects.

Often employees don't feel comfortable telling their manager what they want but I bet that most employees will tell each other, sat around the coffee table when they are moaning about exactly what it is they don't desire too!

Encouraging your workforce to be open about their ambitions, to dream about their future, but to also know that they play a part in sculpting out their future, drives your team towards passion for their work. They will feel they are contributing towards their dream if someone is paying attention to what it is they really desire.

Encouraging your team to share their desires, understanding their desires and setting a culture where they can learn to achieve them puts you on the road to an engaged workforce. Henry George said *"Man is the only animal whose desires increase as they are fed; the only animal that is never satisfied"*.

This is very true, because once a desire is satisfied, we are hungry for more.

As a business leader / manager what you desire will shape your business decisions, it will help you decide on the right path or course of action. Knowing how to prioritise which desires you will aim to satisfy first makes you into a great leader.

Desire will lead to business growth. When have you heard 'if we grow our revenue by 20% this year we will be more profitable', or 'we need to double our turnover in the next 3 years in order to survive' or 'if we can achieve another 50% in sales we will be number 1 in our marketplace'? Probably often?
But then what happens when those companies achieve those goals? They set more goals, bigger goals, they have larger aspirations. They don't feel satisfied with the first goal and think 'oh well we achieved that, so now we'll just retire, shut up shop'. Instead they push on, further and further because the hunger for success is never satisfied.

As a business grows it gains momentum, competitive advantage; it creates value for customers, employees, it gains size and probably assets and net worth. However, achieving that next level only makes you want to push on to a new height, it is driving each business to see where the boundaries are, and as an entrepreneur those boundaries are often limitless.

"If you greatly desire something, have the guts to stake everything on obtaining it."
Brendan Francis

Step 3: Ignite your passion

In order to build a truly engaged workforce you need people to be passionate about their work and their life. You cannot create passion in someone but you can ignite it. What you can do is provide an environment where it's ok to have passion. Whether it is the office junior that has a passion for a clean and tidy stationery cupboard, to an accountant who has passion for numbers or the marketing guru that has a passion to conquer the world with your product offering, it doesn't matter. But having passion is crucial for your business success.

When an employee is working on a project they are passionate about, you will see them put in the extra effort, they will stay later, take on more responsibility, they won't just be clock watching and out the door right on time each day.

If you have been lucky enough to come across some truly passionate employees in your time, you will know what I mean. I am passionate about HR, my style of HR. I get up every morning and I can't wait to turn on my computer and get to work, I love what I do every day and that makes me very happy.

Once you can achieve this, work does not feel like work. I might be accused of being a workaholic, I am truly not; but when I am working I am so engaged and passionate about my work that I enjoy it. Never do I dread getting up on a Monday morning and going to work! Imagine if you could get all your employees into such a euphoric state?

You need to have passion in what you are doing otherwise you will lose interest. Doing something every day that you don't feel passionate about becomes a chore, and you won't stick at it. You need to make sure the activities in your business are born from your passion. Maybe it's a passion for a certain industry, customer service or for helping people. You need to identify what those passions are and hold onto them.

Richard Branson said "When you believe in something the force of your convictions will spark other people's interest and motivate them to help you achieve your goals. This is essential to success." Others around you need to see your passion, they need to know why it is that you get up every day at the crack of dawn, why you're the last one out of the office at night and why you bounce into the office first thing Monday morning, raring to go!

Finding the spark of passion in each and every one of your team members is truly a sign of greatness. If *you* can inspire a young trainee to find their passion and help them pursue it, then you've led.

David Lucatch, founder and CEO of Yappn Corporation says passion is the key to success: "The people I have seen achieve the greatest success in their professional and personal lives are passionate people that lead, support, and mentor others with that 'zeal and zest' for the work and people".

"If there is no passion in your life, then have you really lived? Find your passion, whatever it may be. Become it, and let it become you and you will find great things happen FOR you, TO you and BECAUSE of you."

T Alan Armstrong

Step 4: Create your vision

You may be the manager / business leader and you may have a vision but that vision is nothing without sharing it with everyone else. We often talk in HR about aligning business objectives, strategy and vision, but put simply, it is about letting everyone in your business know where you want to get to, what the end goal is and what's in it for them if they help you get there.

As a business leader you will probably already have a vision of some kind. Really taking time to put this vision down on paper, to set timescales for achieving it, adding milestones or goals will focus your business.

Ask your team for feedback on what their vision is for the company, where would they like to see it be in 1, 3 and 5 years. Don't just settle for mediocre, really push the boundary of your imagination. Having a strong goal in mind identifies you as a strong leader, someone with great aspirations. Your team will look up to this, but do make your goals achievable and realistic.

Everyone if your business needs to know what it is the organization is working towards and then what their contribution is adding to this. If your teams cannot see the reason that their work is important or how their work is contributing towards achieving this vision, then they will become despondent.

When I help my clients I always pose 2 questions about a course of action they are considering taking:

1) Does this course of action make money or save money?
2) Does it create customer or employee satisfaction?

If the answer to either or both is no, then why would you even be considering doing it?

Award winning brand consultant Simon Mainwaring says "Transforming a brand into a socially responsible leader doesn't happen overnight by simply writing new marketing and advertising strategies. It takes effort to identify a vision that your customers will find credible and aligned with their values."[xi] So it is important when creating your vision to consider both your customers and employees.

If your vision does not sit right with their values, then they will not have faith in what you are doing and they certainly won't follow you along the way.

Martin Luther King's infamous "I have a dream speech" nearly didn't have the "I have a dream phrase in it", one of his campaign team wanted to write this out, thank goodness he didn't. In an interesting article by Jesse Lyn Stoner, she says that "a real vision continues to inspire and guide people beyond the lifetime of the person who articulated it".

She also writes about leveraging the physics of change in order to bring about transformation and I highly recommend reading this article here[xii]: http://seapointcenter.com/the-physics-of-change/

If you're struggling to understand the power of a vision, then here's 31 Martin Luther King quotes to help you realise your vision:

http://www.inc.com/marla-tabaka/31-martin-luther-king-jr-quotes-to-inspire-greatness-in-you.html

"Innovation distinguishes between a leader and a follower"

Steve Jobs

Step 5: Have courage to do what it takes to get there

Being a business leader takes courage and being an entrepreneur takes courage. For others just getting up in front of a few colleagues to make a presentation takes courage. No matter what your fear or challenge is, big or small, having the courage to face it and conquer it is what makes you stronger. The confidence and belief you will gain by having the courage to stand up and do what makes you nervous is completely empowering.

Having the courage to take the difficult business decisions when it matters makes a truly great leader. Having those difficult performance conversations, leading change through adversity, getting done what needs to get done takes courage. Not addressing the issues, burying your head in the sand, not addressing bad behaviours or listening to your teams, makes you appear weak. Your team needs you to be strong, to make those bold decisions, they need someone to follow that has the courage to just do what it takes, when it's necessary.

You can demonstrate courage by acting quickly to address poor performance, poor management, poor behaviours. You need to have courage to talk openly with your team about a bad situation and give constructive criticism, then you will earn their respect. If you can earn their respect then they will trust you, they will trust you to lead them to wherever it is that they need to be.

You also need to encourage others to have courage. Remember this is about building a culture within your organization where everyone feels valued and ready to contribute at the highest level they can. You need to encourage the new line manager to stand up and take control. You can also encourage the most nervous employee to open up and give the 360° feedback to their manager. You will need to have authority when you speak so that everyone sits up and listens.

"Courage is what it takes to stand up and speak; courage is also what it takes to sit down and listen."

Winston Churchill

Step 6: Believe in yourself and others

When Richard Branson started selling records to his mates at school, did he believe that he had what it takes to create a global brand as successful as Virgin?

In business you have to believe that you have what it takes, or at least have the people around you that have what it takes. You have to believe in your product, your service and have the courage to stand up and say this is what we believe in. You also have to make your existing and future customers believe in it.

I read a very interesting article by Louise Altman (@intentionalcomm) regarding beliefs in the workplace. You can see the full article here[xiii]: *http://intentionalworkplace.com/2011/05/20/the-power-of-beliefs-at-work/*.

Louise discusses the fact that:

"For adults, workplace cultures play an important role in impacting and reinforcing beliefs. Workplace cultures, which are the aggregate of the emotions, attitudes, beliefs, values, ethics, and behaviours of the people who work there, and the organization itself, are huge transmitters of cultural norms (beliefs). When we are at work, we're usually either swimming in sync with the prevailing beliefs of our group or organization, or fighting an uphill battle against them. Managers and consultants often talk about *alignment* as a critical tool for organizational success. But individual beliefs must first be **self-aligned** before they can be "on board" with the collective goals and values of an organization."

I whole heartedly agree with this statement, so much so that I could not have said it better myself!

The word doctrine is derived from the Ancient Greek word 'doxa' which refers to opinion and acceptance. The reason for having belief is to guide your actions in a particular course, to determine what it is and why it is that you do something. Quite often the workplace can challenge our existing beliefs, things that we thought we knew from an early age and can bring doubt and confusion to our minds. Other beliefs hold us back, simply accepting or believing that we cannot achieve something because our course or path is already pre-determined.

Your role as a business leader is to help change beliefs where necessary. Beliefs control and direct people, they determine how they behave. If we do not challenge a particularly destructive or limiting belief, then we won't progress.

To help others believe in a course of action or a change of direction from what they believe is the right way takes courage; it also takes patience and wisdom. You need to show them the reasons behind your belief, to help them understand why is it you believe they can achieve what is necessary through that particular course of action.

Many people used to believe that lemmings committed mass suicide jumping off cliffs into the water. They held this belief until Ole Worm a natural historian showed that lemmings actually have a migratory desire /need and that they will jump off a cliff and swim to achieve that desire, however many die when they underestimate the duration of the swim.

This misconception about lemmings was widely publicised and many a film has made reference to their 'mass suicide' behaviour. It shows how an assumed belief in something can be wide spread as truth, without any proof. Turn this around though and think about how you can inspire others to follow you in the right way, without any proof that what you believe in is going to work; since in business you do not always know what is going to work or if you are going the right way at the time!

"One person with a belief is equal to a force of 99 who have only interests".
John Stuart Mill

Step 7: Find fortitude in each other

The adversity and challenge that comes with being a manager, entrepreneur or world business leader is immense. You will face daily challenges from small to absolutely business critical, make or break scenarios.

In order to handle these challenges, you need fortitude. To stand there and shake your head and have no clue what to do when presented with a challenge will quickly dissolve your business. To stand there and say "actually, I might not know exactly what we need to do now but I will do everything in my power to find a solution and make us succeed no matter what" shows fortitude.

To come to work every day and deal with situation after situation that is coming to trip you up, but still have a smile on your face and greet every individual like it's a blissful summer's day, takes fortitude. To not crumble under the severity of the situation takes fortitude.

Fortitude, or strength of mind needs to be at the heart of you and your business. Having the perseverance and endurance to see a project through from start to finish, no matter what, is fortitude. Now I am not suggesting that you don't change your course during a project, there will always be changes of direction as you progress, but having the determination to succeed, no matter what, is what counts. You need to demonstrate a great strength for your team, to show them you have the resoluteness to get things done.

Your team may lose heart along the way, but you need to stand strong and support them through it. You need to encourage your managers and team leaders to have fortitude and tenacity. This is where leading by example really counts. If your employees see you or your managers giving up part way through, then they will do the same. You need to find a communal spirit, one that pushes you all on together, find solace in small successes and gains along the way, stand strong and don't give up.

You must recognise the difference between laziness and lack of direction. Sometimes an employee may appear lazy but often they are lacking support and direction from peers or managers. Take time to find out what is really going on around you. Open up channels of communication between senior and junior employees. Hang out around the coffee machine and listen to the casual talk, you will often find out far more about the state of the situation here than you will in a formal review process.

Do you have the mental and emotional strength to stand up and lead your people through all the challenges your business brings? Many attempts to create a change in an organisation either fail completely or at least partially. In a 2013 study, Towers Watson found only 25% of change programmes are sustained over time. Taking your people through a process of change can be a particularly daunting process, and well people are people, they're human and things don't always go according to plan.

Jesse Lyn Stoner states 7 key factors to successfully managing a change project:

1. *The purpose and need for the change must be clear and compelling.*
2. *Show the whole picture – the vision of the end-result AND the roadmap to get there.*
3. *Involve your team and all key stakeholders deeply and early on.*
4. *Senior leaders must demonstrate their commitment.*
5. *The approach to the change effort needs to be consistent with the desired ends.*
6. *Integrate the change work with real work.*
7. *Over communicate.*

Read the full article here[xiv]:
http://seapointcenter.com/why-most-change-efforts-fail/

Keep these 7 key factors in mind when you start introducing the Principles of Greatness and any other change initiative in your business. Remember, change often frightens and unsettles people. You need to be prepared for all manner of negative reactions. On the flip side some people will welcome the change, it could be just what they have been waiting for. You might see some surprisingly positive behaviours that you didn't think possible. Again, it's the human factor and you just can't predict that!

"Fortitude is the marshal of thought, the armour of the will, and the fort of reason."
Francis Bacon

Step 8: Have compassion in your actions

It is so important to show compassion and understanding for others, to put others first and go out of your way to understand how they are feeling. Think of the CEO walking through the office floor with 200 employees who still manages to stop by an employee's desk and ask how their child or partner is, or the manager that goes out of their way to take a team member for a coffee just to see how their health is, even in the busiest of schedules.

Knowing your employees by name, knowing a little about their lives so that you can communicate on a personal level but ultimately giving care and consideration to their personal situations shows compassion. A business needs to care about personal issues, work life balance and understand that an employee is a whole person and that their personal lives, issues and experiences *do* have an impact on how they are at work.

The old way of thinking such as 'don't bring your personal life into work' is hopefully changing. Making it ok to talk about mental health issues, money problems, family problems and helping employees deal with these makes for a compassionate employer. Look into occupational health provisions and confidential employee help (support) phone lines; make it ok to take personal time to deal with issues outside of work; encourage a buddy/mentor system as a support mechanism.

Supporting your employees through difficult times with littles things that make them sit up and go 'wow I didn't expect that' gives a great feel good feeling all around. Expressing your thanks when someone does something more than you expect goes a long way.

A hand written thank you note from a senior manager, even on a post-it note can be enough to tell people you value them.

"If you want others to be happy, practice compassion. If you want to be happy, practice compassion."
The Dalai Lama

Step 9: Act with the utmost integrity at all times

One of the worst things a manager can do to break trust with their team is over promise and under deliver. A manager / leader must demonstrate that they do exactly what they say they are going to do. It's also about setting an example. A manager should not discipline a team member for being late when they themselves are late, where's the fairness in that?

To have ethics and principles at the forefront of your actions shows integrity, to live by and demonstrate your values every day, no matter what, shows integrity. Your employees will value integrity over everything.

One of the most frequent complaints I hear about as an HR professional is about 'bad management'. Examples of this being the manager who is always late for meetings, yet shouts at a team member when they do the same thing; or the manager that disciplines someone for being absent 3 times when another colleague which they 'appear' to like better is late 5 times and nothing is said; or worse still when their own absence record is not exemplary. How about the manager that over promises and never delivers or the one that just doesn't deal with anything? Their team will quickly lose faith and respect.

When a manager makes alliances or appears to make alliances with certain team members over others it quickly becomes noticed in the workplace. Other employees will quickly recognise that an employee is being treated more favourably than others and this breeds resentment.

Team members will very quickly lose trust and faith in the manager that sides with one employee over others. How can a manager who is late or frequently absent themselves have the respect of team members to preside over the discipline of others in the same situation?

One of the worst things a manager can do is lie to a team member or promise to do something that they have absolutely no intention of doing. As a manager / leader you must set the best example to everyone around you.

You must act at all times with the utmost professionalism. You must be where you say you will be, on time; you must be present when you say you will be present; you must deliver on the promises you make to team members; if there's a policy in your organisation for something then don't violate this policy, even if you are the boss!

Your employees need someone to look up to, someone they can trust and respect to do the right thing at all times, someone beyond reproach. Employees don't leave companies, they leave managers.

If team leaders / managers in your business are not acting with integrity then your employees will soon tell you, with their resignations!

It is a lot easier to have trust in someone that has never done anything to break that trust than it is to have to regain trust in someone that has let you down. Employees won't easily forget the actions of negligent managers and they certainly won't be productive for them.

"The supreme quality for leadership is unquestionably integrity. Without it, no real success is possible, no matter whether it is on a section gang, a football field, in an army, or in an office."

Dwight D. Eisenhower

Step 10: Find wisdom in others

In your business you should make it your priority to learn about every area, every department, every employee. You should do your research and learn about a problem before making a decision. Consulting others in your business for their opinions shows wisdom.

Ultimately as a business leader the decision may be yours, but it is your responsibility to make wise decisions. If you don't always make the right decision you must have the courage to be honest about this, reflect upon what went wrong, then use this knowledge to move forward: this is wisdom.

I love the fact that people refer every day to 'common sense' and yet we see people so often not using 'common sense' and doing things which to the onlooker appear ridiculous. But just stop and think for a moment, if someone has never experienced a particular situation, or has not been shown a way of doing things or has not observed a parent completing a similar task then how are they supposed to know what to do?

I don't believe in common sense in the most part, I believe we learn through teaching or experience of situations. You cannot just magic knowledge into your head and therefore common sense or the acquisition of common sense is really about the gathering (either consciously or subconsciously) of knowledge and then applying that knowledge to problem solve in future situations.

The accumulation of knowledge does not have value unless you can apply that knowledge. We need to use the knowledge ethically and morally, with compassion and kindness, with integrity and respect. Respecting and acknowledging different viewpoints and allowing others to present their opinions before making a judgment shows wisdom. Having the understanding of how your actions will affect those around you and being mindful of your words towards others shows wisdom. A wise person listens and thinks before acting.

The people in your business will be looking towards you for words of wisdom as you move your organisation forward. You need to seek out the knowledge, listen for the indicators from around your business and then act with integrity when you decide the appropriate course of action.

If the course of action doesn't go 100% according to plan that's ok, that's how we learn, but you need to be honest with people and have the courage to stand up and change what needs to be changed to get back on course.

"If we choose only to expose ourselves to opinions and viewpoints that are in line to our own, we become more polarized, more set in our own ways. It will only reinforce and deepen the political divides in our country. But if we choose to actively seek out information that challenges our assumptions and beliefs, perhaps we can begin to understand where the people who disagree with us are coming from."
Barack Obama

Let's recap at how we take the Principles of Greatness into our business:

Step 1: Set out your values

Step 2: Share your desires

Step 3: Create your vision

Step 4: Have courage to do what it takes to get there

Step 5: Ignite your passion

Step 6: Believe in yourself and others

Step 7: Find fortitude in each other

Step 8: Have compassion in your actions

Step 9: Act with the utmost integrity at all times

Step 10: Find wisdom in others

What is your doctrine?

In the early Middle Ages, the King would make a proclamation and send his representatives out across the land to decree to the people. That was a top down approach where the decree was an official order that had the force of the law of the King behind it. In 1215 King John had to agree a charter of liberty and political rights with his barons at Runnymede and forthwith was born the English constitutional practice.

We pride ourselves in the UK in living in a democracy, where the views of the people matter and politicians serve the people and are held accountable. So why in so many modern day businesses do the managers and HR professionals set the rules, policies and procedures?

Well hopefully more and more businesses are now seeing the benefits of a truly collaborative approach, where all colleagues have a voice, a method of communication that can really effect change in their organisation.

We do however have to take care to reinforce this, by whatever means possible in your organisation. But take heed, creating an employee voice mechanism and not taking it seriously or not acting upon it breeds contempt. You must truly believe in the knowledge, wisdom and judgement of all your employees and the contribution they offer to your organisation's success.

The Company Charter

One simple tool I suggest is the Company Charter. By setting out your doctrine, the way you want your business to exist in a simple Company Charter that is visible to all parts of the organisation, you can remind everyone each day of what success looks like for your business.

Your doctrine is simple, it is the basis of how you do business, every day, in everything you do. So what does a Company Charter look like? Here's an example to get you started, you can modify it as you wish:

1. We live by our values
2. We respect everyone
3. We're honest with each other
4. We acknowledge areas of development needs
5. We empower everyone
6. We recognise and celebrate differences
7. We reward behaviours as well as achievement
8. We lead from the front, back and sides
9. We set an example to our colleagues, customers and industry
10. And... We follow the principles of greatness every day, in everything we do

"A good cult delivers on its promises. A good cult nourishes the needs of its members, has transparency and integrity, and creates provisions for challenging its leadership openly. A good cult expands the freedoms and well-being of its members rather than limits them."
Philip Zimbardo

Conclusion

"Your time is limited, so don't waste it living someone else's life. Don't be trapped by dogmas, which is living with the results of other people's thinking. Don't let the noise of other's opinions drown out your inner voice. And most important, have the courage to follow your heart and intuition. They already know what you truly want to become. Everything else is secondary"
Steve Jobs

To be a truly inspirational leader and create a great workplace where everyone wants to be, you must be truly engaged yourself.

You need to be passionate about your business, your people, your customers.

You need to find the very reason that makes you jump out of bed every day and rush into work. You need to be the one that smiles every day, you need to be the positive, strong influence in the workplace.

Your people will not follow a moody, irritable, changeable boss that lacks drive, direction or confidence!

You need to find your direction, establish your vision, share it with everyone, become resilient and lead on where others can follow.

Do you think that Steve Jobs got to where he did by being mediocre?

Think big, act big, break the mould and shake things up.

Don't worry about the moaners and groaners who will always try to put a downer on things, show them the Principles of Greatness and ask them to take a long hard look at themselves. If they don't get on board straight away, show them again, if they still don't get on board then your organisation is not the right place for them; you'll need to have courage to have that conversation.

You need to surround yourself with like-minded people, recognise your strengths and weaknesses, work hard on improving those weaknesses, find the positives in every scenario, don't dwell on the negatives.

Find your spirit, make the most of now, show your individuality, but also demonstrate your similarities with your team.

Strive to do every the very best that you can, 2nd best is not an option.

Excellence will become the norm. You will be the shining example to the rest of your team.

Remember people don't often leave jobs, they leave bosses. Your leadership must demonstrate why it is people should stay within your business.

You are going to give your people a place to thrive, grow, contribute, relate, have autonomy and ultimately enjoy being.

You are going to establish a truly great place to work where the Principles of Greatness will guide each and every person.

The Principles of Greatness are your foundations, once you have laid the foundations you can go on and build a great business.

You have the foundations, what will you build today?

"Here's to the crazy ones, the misfits, the rebels, the troublemakers, the round pegs in the square holes... the ones who see things differently -- they're not fond of rules... You can quote them, disagree with them, glorify or vilify them, but the only thing you can't do is ignore them because they change things... they push the human race forward, and while some may see them as the crazy ones, we see genius, because the ones who are crazy enough to think that they can change the world, are the ones who do."

Steve Jobs
(1955 - 2011)

Additional Resources

I know how hard it can be to deliver a new message to line managers, I've been there. Trying to deliver a training session or new concept in a meeting or classroom style seminar can be a little daunting and if you get it wrong it becomes boring and they are in danger of switching off, falling asleep and missing your message entirely!

I know what it's like to read a great book at the weekend, feel completely inspired and then go rushing into the office and tell everyone about it only to have blank stares facing back at you as you go waffling on without any context whatsoever and you feel like a complete idiot!

So don't worry, just do your best, make a start and get the message out there.

You can download a PDF list of websites, books and other publications as additional resources from my Members Resources area of my website. I will be adding to this as I increase the number of my publications.

I have also included a list of 21 FREE employee engagement ideas for you. These ideas are FREE to implement in your business, no need to spend a fortune, just some simple ideas that you could implement right away.

Please visit:
http://www.myhrbusinesspartner.co.uk/#!blank/cdsy

Author Thank You

Thank you so much for purchasing my book. I hope that you have enjoyed reading this book as much I enjoyed writing it. If you've enjoyed this book, please let me know by leaving an Amazon rating and a brief review! It only takes a minute and I read all my reviews. It's really useful to me as an independent author and helps others to find my work. I am always interested to hear from my readers and you can contact me directly at:

Email: adele@myhrbusinesspartner.co.uk.
Twitter: @myhrbp
Linkedin: https://uk.linkedin.com/in/adele-marsh-mcipd-5a601b18

I do hope you have taken away some useful information that you can put into practice in your own business. My HR Bites Series books are designed to be useful workplace guides ensuring that you can get the best out of yourself, your people and your work life.

I very much enjoy questions from my readers and if you would like to get in touch directly drop me an email or tweet me @myhrbp. I would love to hear how you get on with implementing the Principles of Greatness in your business and your success stories with improving employee engagement.

Get notified of forthcoming publications, free book downloads and beta reading opportunities by signing up to my book mailing list here:

http://eepurl.com/b1PKIL

Until next time and wishing you every success in your business, Adele Marsh

About the Author

Adele Marsh MCIPD is an experienced HR Business Partner that has nearly 20 years of HR and operational management experience in E-commerce, Digital, Late night leisure, Licensed Trade and Contact Centre sectors.

Following 5 years as an HR Operations Director in a start up that grew to over £1.1m turnover in just over 3 years, Adele decided to specialise in Human Resource Management and undertook her Professional Assessment of Competence Level 7 qualification with the Chartered Institute of Personnel and Development to gain Chartered Membership in 2012.

Following this Adele spent 18 months in Northern Ireland as a successful HR Business Partner for Teleperformance, a global contact centre organisation employing over 130,000 staff across 258 sites. Adele had responsibility for up to 450 employees. Moving back to England towards the end of 2013, Adele spent 6 months as an HR Consultant for Practical HR before deciding move into consultancy fulltime, founding My HR Business Partner.

As a professional Human Resources Consultant and business leader, Adele has experience working at a senior level, engaging with board members, directors and CEOs.

Adele has a wealth of experience delivering both strategic and operational advice and guidance across all aspects of HRD including: Employee Relations, Engagement, Reward, Resourcing, Performance Management, Talent management, Succession Planning, Organisational Development and Change Management.

Adele has a high level of communication and influencing skills to coach, challenge and provide advice stakeholders at all levels. Adele has also been successful in writing & implementing Policies & Procedures across the full HR spectrum in both existing & new organisations, along with a successful track record in Management Development.

Adele has a very strong operational background with excellent leadership skills and experience of working in matrix organisations.

Adele is an avid promoter of the #FOW (future of work) and positive disruption of workplace culture. A keen interest in employee engagement and high performing work cultures.

In 2015 Adele decided to pursue her passion for writing and is now penning various HR related books, under the 'HR Bites Series' through My HR Business Partner Publishing. Adele is a great believer in self-motivation, striving for excellence and supporting others to do the same. Her writings are intended to be informative, practical and implementable in any business.

Adele can be contacted directly at adele@myhrbusinesspartner.co.uk or on twitter @myhrbp

References

i http://www.personneltoday.com/hr/employee-engagement-are-your-happy-workers-disengaged/

ii Fowler, Susan (2014-09-30). Why Motivating People Doesn't Work . . . and What Does: The New Science of Leading, Energizing, and Engaging. Berrett-Koehler Publishers. Kindle Edition.

iii Fowler, Susan (2014-09-30). Why Motivating People Doesn't Work . . . and What Does: The New Science of Leading, Energizing, and Engaging. Berrett-Koehler Publishers. Kindle Edition.

iv Hagel, John III, Passion versus ambition: Did Steve Jobs have worker passion? Deloitte University Press, November 19, 2014, http:// dupress.com/articles/employee-passionambition/'?coll=6211

v http://www.cipd.co.uk/binaries/employee-outlook_2015-spring.pdf

vi *Company as Community 2015:* https://s3.amazonaws.com/bestworkplacesdb/publications/WO_2015_BestWorkplaces_en.pdf

vii http://www.greatplacetowork.co.uk/our-services/assess-your-organisation/workplace-culture-assessment

viii http://primalstrengthcamp.com/finding-your-swagger/

ix https://en.wikipedia.org/w/index.php?title=Wisdom&oldid=7002518 15

x ttp://www.greatplacetowork.co.uk/storage/documents/organisational%20values%20are%20they%20worth%20the%20bother%20final2%20web%20031114.pdf

xi http://mashable.com/2011/04/22/csr-company-stages/#2wMBmhlGzqqo

xii http://seapointcenter.com/the-physics-of-change/

xiii *http://intentionalworkplace.com/2011/05/20/the-power-of-beliefs-at-work/*

www.ingramcontent.com/pod-product-compliance
Lightning Source LLC
Chambersburg PA
CBHW060403190526
45169CB00002B/726